Published by Creative Education and
Creative Paperbacks
P.O. Box 227, Mankato, Minnesota 56002
Creative Education and Creative Paperbacks
are imprints of The Creative Company
www.thecreativecompany.us

Design by The Design Lab
Production by Chelsey Luther
Printed in the United States of America

Photographs by Corbis (Tim Davis, Frans Lanting,
Ocean, Monica & Michael Sweet/Design Pics), Getty
Images (Pete Atkinson, Georgette Douwma, James
Urbach), Shutterstock (abcphotosystem, foryouinf,
idreamphoto, Isabelle Kuehn, Neophuket, Burhan
Bunardi Xie)

Library of Congress Cataloging-in-Publication Data
Riggs, Kate.
Sea turtles / Kate Riggs.
p. cm. — (Amazing animals)
Summary: A basic exploration of the appearance,
behavior, and habitat of sea turtles, the migrating
shelled reptiles. Also included is a story from folklore
explaining how sea turtles cause monsoons.
Includes index.
ISBN 978-1-60818-491-0 (hardcover)
ISBN 978-1-62832-091-6 (pbk)
1. Sea turtles—Juvenile literature. I. Title. II. Series:
Amazing animals.
QL666.C536R556 2015
597.92'8—dc23   2013051252

CCSS: RI.1.1, 2, 4, 5, 6, 7; RI.2.2, 5, 6, 7, 10;
RI.3.1, 5, 7, 8; RF.1.1, 3, 4; RF.2.3, 4

First Edition
9 8 7 6 5 4 3 2 1

AMAZING ANIMALS

SEA TURTLES

BY KATE RIGGS

CREATIVE EDUCATION • CREATIVE PAPERBACKS

Most sea turtles stay in the water except when they nest

Sea turtles are **reptiles** with shells. There are seven kinds of sea turtles. They live in warm waters around the world.

reptiles animals that have scales and bodies that are always as warm or as cold as the air around them

Sea turtles' shells are not as rounded as tortoises' shells are. This helps turtles swim more easily. Sea turtles have powerful legs for swimming, too. Their feet are called flippers.

Sea turtles cannot pull their head into their shell

Leatherbacks are the largest sea turtles. They can weigh 2,000 pounds (907 kg)! That is heavier than any other reptile in the world. Ridley sea turtles are much smaller. They weigh 80 to 100 pounds (36.3–45.4 kg).

Leatherbacks have rubbery shells with ridges, or bumps

Sea turtles live in water, but they breathe air. They can hold their breath for a few minutes to look for food. Or they can stay underwater for a long time to sleep. Green sea turtles can hold their breath for five hours.

*Hawksbill sea turtles
have a pair of claws
on each flipper*

Jellyfish and about 95 percent of all animals lack backbones

Sea turtles use their beaks to grab food. They do not have teeth. Most sea turtles eat small **ocean** or sea animals. They like to eat fish, clams, crabs, and jellyfish. Adult green sea turtles eat plants.

ocean a big area of deep, salty water

Many sea turtles nest on the same beach where they were born

Female sea turtles lay their eggs on a beach. The eggs open after two or three months. The **hatchlings** dig themselves out of the sandy nest. They cross the beach to the water as fast as they can.

hatchlings baby sea turtles

Seabirds and crabs are **predators** of hatchlings. Sea turtles in the water sometimes get caught in fishing nets. The largest sea turtles can live for a long time. Some live as long as 150 years.

predators animals that kill and eat other animals

Green sea turtles are named for their greenish skin

Sea turtles swim near the surface to warm up. They dive to deeper water when they need to cool down. They **migrate** to find food or mates. Leatherbacks travel more than 3,000 miles (4,828 km) a year.

migrate move from place to place during different parts of the year

People can see turtles on land when the females lay eggs. Some people help hatchlings reach the sea. It can be fun to watch tiny turtles dart across the sand!

Sea turtles are endangered, meaning there are not many left

A Sea Turtle Story

What causes storms known as monsoons? People in India say that a sea turtle swims under the world. It carries four elephants on its shell. The elephants hold up the world. The turtle swims around and makes waves in the ocean. When it splashes, it makes bigger waves and moves the wind. The wind brings rainy monsoons to India.

Read More

Herriges, Ann. *Sea Turtles*. Minneapolis: Bellwether Media, 2007.

Marsh, Laura. *Sea Turtles*. Washington, D.C.: National Geographic, 2011.

Websites

Turtle Tides for Kids
http://www.conserveturtles.org/turtletides.php
Download activities, look at pictures, or play games about sea turtles.

Turtle Voyager Game
http://www.pbs.org/wnet/nature/episodes/voyage-of-the-lonely-turtle
/turtle-voyager-game/4099/
Help a loggerhead turtle travel across the ocean and learn more about sea turtles.

Note: Every effort has been made to ensure that the websites listed above are suitable for children, that they have educational value, and that they contain no inappropriate material. However, because of the nature of the Internet, it is impossible to guarantee that these sites will remain active indefinitely or that their contents will not be altered.